Then & **Now**

CHESHIRE SALT COUNTRY

Crowds assembled in 1901 at the Bull Ring at Northwich, then the place of general assembly for all big occasions in the town, to hear the proclamation of King Edward VII. Today, the covered facilities at the Memorial Hall are used for meetings, which are much safer as the Bull Ring is now a busy cross roads and totally unsuitable for public gatherings!

Then & Now
CHESHIRE SALT COUNTRY

COMPILED BY J. BRIAN CURZON

TEMPUS

ACKNOWLEDGEMENTS

The inspiration for this record of how mid Cheshire looks, compiled in the year of Queen Elizabeth II's Golden Jubilee Year, came from John Henry Cook, whose own home at Crossfield backed onto my childhood home. His *Queen's Diamond Jubilee in Cheshire* is a fascinating record of the 1897 Jubilee. His book was accepted by the Queen, but dare I claim one-upmanship as I was introduced to Her Majesty during her Jubilee tour?

Companion books for the period are T.A. Coward, *Picturesque Cheshire* of 1903 (Sherrat and Hughes) and Fletcher Moss, *Pilgrimages to Old Homes* 1902. There is no contemporary account, although the author's *Hidden Cheshire* tells some obscure tales, guide books from the Borough and Town Councils provide details of local services.

The Winsford Local History Society have very kindly allowed more of their old photographs to be used. The *Mid Cheshire Chronicle* have, as always, helped with copies of old photographs to fill in the gaps. The interior view of British Salt's production at Middlewich was provided by the company, otherwise all modern photos are by the author.

First published 2003

Tempus Publishing Limited
The Mill, Brimscombe Port,
Stroud, Gloucestershire, GL5 2QG

© Brian Curzon, 2003

The right of J. Brian Curzon to be identified as the Author of this work has been asserted in accordance with the Copyrights, Designs and Patents Act 1988.

British Library Cataloguing in Publication Data.
A catalogue record for this book is available from the British Library.

ISBN 0 7524 2675 3

Typesetting and origination by Tempus Publishing Limited
Printed in Great Britain by Midway Colour Print, Wiltshire

The late Victorian and Edwardian periods were ones for assemblies; there was no television to keep people at home and crowds would assemble for almost anything unusual. In this picture John Brunner (wearing a white top hat in his carriage, bottom left) was met by his workforce after a world tour in 1887. The workmen took his horses from the carriage and pulled it themselves to show respect.

Winnington Hall is used today as a venue for weddings and other gatherings as well as a conference centre.

INTRODUCTION

When an invitation to prepare a 'then and now' book arrived, the memory of the Millennium was still fresh and the Golden Jubilee was just a few weeks away. Almost a century before, John Henry Cooke – Winsford's indomitable first Town Clerk – would have been putting the finishing touches to his book *Queen's Diamond Jubilee in Cheshire*. So why not look at that golden era a century ago and compare it with today?

It was a great age for celebrating. Queen Victoria's Golden Jubilee in 1887 and Diamond Jubilee in 1897 were followed closely by the dawn of the twentieth century, the Boer War and the Accession and Coronation of Edward VII in 1902. Before he became King Edward, 'Bertie' had a strong link to Mid Cheshire and visited this area. He came to hunt with the Cheshire Hounds at Sandiway, visited The Brockhurst at Leftwich and stayed with his friend the Earl of Enniskillen at Hartford Grange, where lavish parties were held.

Local industrial philanthropists Sir John Brunner and the Verdin Family richly endowed the towns which were growing around their works, and were friends with King Edward who surrounded himself with the wealthy industrialists and politicians of the age. It was to become known as 'La Belle Epoch' (the beautiful age) for it all came to an end in 1914 with the advent of the First World War.

It is often impossible to tell exactly when a photograph was taken but, as far as is possible to tell, all the old pictures in this book were taken before the First World War. All the modern images were captured in the summer of Queen Elizabeth's Golden Jubilee. John Henry compiled a thick volume describing all the events held in Cheshire to mark Victoria's Jubilee. For the 2002 Jubilee many people chose to watch the events in London on television in the comfort of their own homes; something which would have been impossible in Victorian times.

It is interesting to compare Cooke's accounts of the 1897 Jubilee to the situation today. Then arches of salt, chemicals, barrels and even of bicycles and crates for condensed milk marked the local industries. Amongst the events which marked the day, the elderly inmates at the workhouse in London Road at Northwich were given a special Jubilee tea with cakes and fruit pies. It would have been nice to mark this with a pair of pictures, but no one felt it was worth taking a photograph of the workhouse in 1897.

It may well have been a 'Belle Epoch' in the country houses around the district but in the towns it was very different. To get a sample of the atmosphere of the time simply read the two books published 100 years ago where T.A. Coward and Fletcher Moss, who both knew the grim reality of life in Manchester, wrote about their visits to the area. They would take a train to one station, cycle around part of Cheshire on a summer's day and then return from a different station. Of Winsford, Fletcher Moss described 'the long filthy hill to Over... it could hardly have been worse than it is; the sun is darkened by the smoke, the stench is horrible: what should be fields are tracts of blackened slime where the skeletons of the trees stand gaunt and withered'. Today, the road through Winsford is, for the most part, a pleasant, tree-lined dual carriageway, more like driving through a wood than a town in mid summer.

Coward commented 'From Winsford Station to Salterswall is practically one long town... along the

Weaver north of Winsford I see the smoke from the brine-pans smoking'. Now, instead of a forest of around 1,000 chimneys, the valley is being planted as part of the new Mersey Forest project.

In old photographs, whenever there is a crowd scene, it is almost always men who are assembled around a subsidence or other feature. Women normally appear in formal shots where they were assembled in their best clothes to accompany men at opening ceremonies, or are included casually standing on the steps of their houses which are being recorded by the Brine Compensation Board. Women then did not have the vote, and, for most, work prospects were limited to a job in the factory or to being 'in service' until they married. Then they would look after children and grandchildren for the rest of their lives.

A century ago, the three salt towns were administered as separate Urban Districts with their own Council and a Rural Council serving the villages around them. Now, they are, for the most part, merged into one Authority called – rather neutrally – Vale Royal, which links Northwich and Winsford. Middlewich was left out and is now part of the Borough of Congleton. It belongs with the other salt towns and has been included as part of 'The Salt Country'. A hundred years ago, the one thing that would have struck people who visited the area was the unity of appearance. In all of the towns and most of the villages there would have been vast sheds containing salt pans steaming away, with chimneys pouring smoke into the atmosphere to mix with the steam and create a foggy haze which only cleared on Mondays; as no one worked on a Sunday. Then the women rushed to get their washing out. The salt industry is illustrated in the Salt Museum (and the decor of many local pubs!) and is only included here to illustrate change.

In Queen Victoria's time, the working classes lived in areas distinct from their middle and upper class betters, in rows of terraced houses near the factory gates. There was little contact between the two ways of life except when a girl from a working-class family left school to live as a servant in a great house or when the gentry attended church or presented some 'improving' gift.

I make no apologies for the fact that some of the photographs will have appeared before in print. The idea is not to show you a different set of photographs for curiosity, but to show the changes that have taken place over a century. Change has sometimes been so dramatic that it is impossible to show the same thing again and sometimes I have reflected this in the photographs I have chosen to take as the 'now'.

I have arranged the book as a visual tour through the Salt district 100 years ago and the same tour taken today. Follow the route yourself, take the book with you and you can find all the places and see for yourselves just how much has changed. Decide for yourself if you think the changes have all been for the better. It is also interesting to ponder on what, if anything will be recognised should someone try to follow this route in the year 2103 or even 3003!

Imagine that you are coming from Manchester by steam train to arrive at Lostock station with your bike, then ride around on a hot July day before returning to Manchester from the Greenbank Station at Hartford. Happy touring!

J. Brian Curzon
November 2002

Northwich and Winsford owed much of their traditional timber-framed architecture to the problems which occured when salt was mined in Northwich and pumped in Winsford. In both towns the ground would sink, taking brick buildings with it. The road outside was raised to bring it back to the old level and keep traffic moving but Parr's shop shows what an unfortunate effect this had on the buildings next to the road. An alternative was to build in timber-frame construction with wood-lined walls. These buildings could be lifted to new road level, as is illustrated in this tailor's shop in the Bull Ring at Northwich.

There is sometimes confusion when people write about the salt industry as they often describe any salt manufacturing place as a salt mine, often writing about Roman or medieval salt mines when there were no such things. Rock salt is a natural mineral found deep underground and was only discovered in 1670, it is mined in the same way as coal, but from much thicker beds, as shown in the picture with the pit pony. Salt was usually made in salt works where rock salt was dissolved in water underground, pumped to the surface, and then boiled in large metal pans to make table salt, as

shown in the picture of a man filling 'peg top' baskets called 'barrows'.

If our imaginary cyclist arrived in the Salt Country from Manchester 100 years ago at Lostock Station, he would realise that the countryside had changed as he came into Lostock. Salt-based chemical works that had started to line the railway here would have been all around as they probably stopped at the Slow and Easy or the Black Greyhound for refreshment. Today it is a busy cross-roads, the Black Greyhound has moved to a new site and the 'Slow' has been rebuilt. A Chinese take-away restaurant stands on one corner, a luxury unimagined in 1897.

Even after there was a regular train service from Lostock, people preferred to catch the regular horse-drawn omnibus which collected people from around the area on its way to Northwich Market. It is shown here at the Black Greyhound. The horse-drawn service was replaced by the North Western motor buses after the First World War. The pub's licence was transferred to a new site at Wincham when the licensing justices decided that there was no need for two pubs so close together. A sports car has replaced the coach and horses and flags fly to support England in the World Cup.

A right turn would follow the Roman Road towards Warrington. On one side, the smoke and steam of the Salt Country would be thick in the air and on the other side, Great Budworth sat on its hillside. It had been much rebuilt in the mid-Victorian era by Squire Egerton Warburton of Arley; but retains the initial appearance of a medieval village. The view is much the same, although it was difficult to recreate it exactly as finding somewhere to park was a problem. Potatoes were still growing on the hill to the left of the village and you can still clearly see the medieval bank which separated the ancient village from the fields on the crest of the hill.

This watercolour of Great Budworth in the late nineteenth century is in Arley Hall and shows a street busy with the affairs of an estate village. Cattle walk down the hill, villagers trail from 'The Running Pump' with buckets of water – three of them are shown in what was then a daily ritual, probably unchanged for centuries. No one carries water in Budworth's affluent streets any more. Although its buildings have hardly changed it is a popular residential area for those who can afford it. Today, you are more likely to meet with cars than cows and the fact that the medieval plan did not provide for garages results

in them parking in the main street and adding to congestion.

Arley Hall is seen through the covered space between the two old barns in the grounds. The rather over-sized Victorian mansion was the centre for a social scene that included hunting, shooting and fishing as the chief pastimes for a weekend house party in Victorian and Edwardian times.

The modern view reveals that the stable yard has become the car parking area for visitors to the house and gardens. It has become a minor television star in its own right as it is often used as a setting for programmes made in Manchester.

The Belle Epoch is captured in this informal picture of part of the gardens at Arley Hall. The lady in the long frilly dress with an enormous hat is gathering summer roses in a basket. Behind her, more sternly dressed women – probably the governess and a lady's maid – are talking to a young girl in their charge, a contrast to some of the pictures of the salt towns! The modern view shows how the old dining hall and rooms for servants were demolished to make a more manageable house. Today, carefully designed replacements provide modern living in a Victorian setting.

'No cartway save on sufferance here' says the sign, but we can proceed down the bridle path to Arley Green and on to High Legh and Mere. Squire Rowland Egerton Warburton of Arley was known as the rhyming squire and had rhyming sign posts erected all over the estates. Although now very much a rural area, Arley deserves to be included as in the eighteenth century the Warburtons first objected to and then took the lead in the Weaver Navigation, becoming rich on the profits to be had from the salt transport.

We continue our journey along the same road back towards Lostock and turn to pass through Marston. The Adelaide Mine was named after Queen Victoria's aunt, the wife of William IV. Underground are railway lines on which round tubs filled with rock salt were pulled to the shaft by pit ponies; men use pick axes, crowbars and shovels to dig away at the rock face. The mine collapsed in 1928 and rock salt mining now takes place at Winsford. The result of the collapse is a circular pool marking the limits of the underground excavation. Instead of salt-miners, it is now the haunt of anglers and wild fowl.

The Cock Inn stands close to the point at which Witton Street becomes Station road – the modern street signs leave a little 'no man's land' between the two! The pub was once at the hub of an area of industrial housing with the town's clay pipe factory in the middle. Today that is replaced by a sheltered housing project opened in 1977 and called Queen Elizabeth house in the Silver Jubilee year. The present building has a fine mosaic of a fighting cock for a sign, and stands alone on a little traffic island.

Next to the mine, the Lion Salt Works are busy with a barge filled with glistening common salt fresh from the pans. The entire workforce has turned out to be photographed. By the hand cart, on the jetty from which salt was tipped into the boat, is a man in salt workers shorts and clogs. Despite its status as a listed building, the works looks semi-derelict as it waits for funding for complete restoration. Now pleasure boats tie up to visit the little museum in the office, while the modern New Cheshire Salt Works can be seen on the other side of the canal.

No one could ever predict where subsidence would occur, wild brine was pumped everywhere until controlled pumping was introduced in the 1920s. No one knew where the brine streams ran and so could not predict where land would collapse. In this dramatic picture, the subsidence took place right under the Trent and Mersey Canal and the water drained into the cavity. It was not possible to take an exact replica, but as the canal was drained and under repair at Anderton it seemed most appropriate to show the way that modern engineering tackled the problem of a canal burst on the same waterway in 2002.

John Brunner gave land for a Free Library, but as street frontage was at a premium, there was only an entrance hall flanked by two shops with the library standing behind. Subsidence destroyed the old brick library which was replaced by a timber-framed building resembling an Elizabethan manor house. Today it sits in an attractive shopping square with ramps provided for wheelchairs resembling those on an ancient temple. Who, 100 years ago, could imagine sitting under a tree in the main street of Northwich?

This arch, with plinths made of salt cut into rusticated blocks to resemble building stone, and the salt blocks which came from the tubs in the right shape for making arches, has the Verdin coat of arms. This shows that it was set up to mark the opening of the Verdin Technical Schools in 1897 which themselves marked Queen Victoria's Diamond Jubilee. The same shops survive, but all that is between them has changed. Again the pleasant pedestrian shopping area of which Northwich is so proud has replaced a narrow cobbled street.

Many old postcards of Northwich show the town's buildings leaning at strange angles. This is a typical example, included simply because it is possible to show the building on the right in a similar photograph today. Note the steps up to the side door; most older Northwich property had several steps to allow the building to sink with subsidence before it needed attention. The brick building has been replaced twice since this postcard was sent, but modern shops in Northwich still occupy the same plots of land shown on eighteenth-century maps.

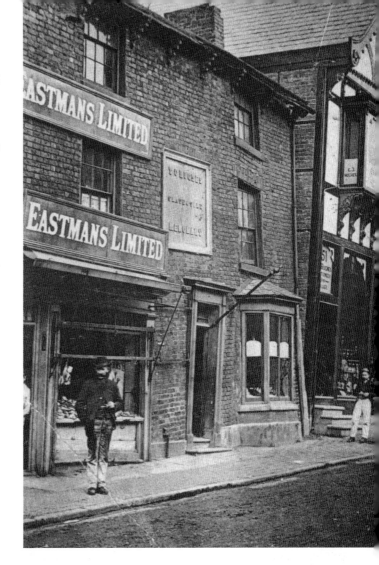

Leading off Witton Street are Leicester Street and Tabley Street, reminders of the former Lords of the Manor, the Leicesters of Tabley Hall. It was built to be substantial working class housing in the early nineteenth century, but by the end of the century had become run down and was demolished in slum clearance schemes of the twentieth century. An exact replica shot was not possible, but this picture shows how what was once a rough side street has been transformed into a busy shopping street giving access to the pedestrianised town-centre from one of the principal car parks.

D espite the quaint appearance of this card, most of the buildings in this view would be comparatively new 100 years ago. Although it still has an Elizabethan appearance, there is nothing in Witton Street that is much older than the period covered by the old photographs in this book, yet many shops of the period have been rebuilt over the last fifty years. Elam's clock in the distance was an Edwardian landmark now replaced by one on Boot's modern store.

One is left to wonder how this photograph of Market Street could be taken at 1.25 (presumably) p.m. according to the clock, and yet not show any shoppers! The shops have clothing, carpets and footwear all clearly on show outside and yet only one boy and a couple of shadowy figures in the distance can be seen. The shops and old market hall have long since been demolished and a bright modern covered market with a 1960s market hall beyond still flourish.

arket Street continued into Crown Street and were both busy shopping streets until the 1960s. Cobble stones, a gas light, enamelled metal trades signs and adverts for butter at 1s and tea at 1s 8d per pound set the tone for this period photograph, as does the milk churn and the shop owner in a white apron in the porch. Crown Street still exists with The Crown at the end, the pub was rebuilt in the 1930s but the rest was redeveloped in the '60s. Car parks, a travel agent and women shopping in track suits are just some of the features that would not be recognised by our 1897 visitor.

Some of the first smiles recorded locally! Victorian photograph's long exposure times made it difficult to record a natural smile, so these two happy shop assistants are a pleasant exception. The shops are typical of old Northwich as they have no upper floor, shop owners chose to live out of town to avoid risks of fire and floods, not to mention smells. However, they have not sunk below the road level, it has been raised in front of them by tipping earth and waste. The names of the shop owners enabled the modern picture of the same addresses to be taken. The buildings have been replaced as they were only made of lightweight plank construction, and today a tree grows outside.

The Bull Ring was the traditional centre of events in Northwich. Until the road improvements in the latter half of the twentieth century people would gather here for community singing at Christmas and New Year and for all public events. High Street was a busy road and lorries still came this way until the 1960s. Notice the old pub sign with barrels and bunches of grapes. Any heavy traffic today has to turn off into the rear access road by the riverside as no traffic of any sort passes down High Street or Witton Street. On the left the road was widened when new shops were built, only to be made narrow again when pedestrianisation took place forty years ago.

No book on old Northwich would be complete without this building with its thatched roof and distinctive upper windows. Older people remember it as Joe Allman's Old Curiosity Shop – crammed with second-hand goods. According to tradition, during the Civil War General Brereton made his home in the house when the hill above was his headquarters. Many regret that the oldest building to survive in Northwich was demolished to make way for a car park. The sign by the barber's pole says 'hair cutting, shaving, shampooing rooms'.

Winnington Hill is still a steep narrow road into the town from the cliffs above where Brereton had his Civil War camp. The photographer was a real novelty and people stand in the road to be pictured. The modern picture was taken on a Sunday as it is too dangerous to stand on the bridge on any other day! The rounded roof is on the former offices of the Marshall family's salt empire. In 2002 it was replaced by homes for the elderly.

Winnington Hill takes us to Winnington, an industrial village built in the grounds of Winnington Hall. These pretty lodges and trees remained at the entrance to the former park of the Hall where Brunner and Mond set up their chemical factory in 1874. In 1897, despite the existence of the factory, much of the park-like aspect of Winnington survived. The lodges have gone and in their place is an entrance road into the busy chemical works with traffic lights and a pair of gas storage tanks.

A romantic view of the river at Winnington. Sailing ships could travel to the works and took the products to all parts of Britain and Europe by water. It was this opportunity for water trade that in Victorian times made Winnington ideal for a factory, but water trade declined in the era of the motor lorry. Today the wharf still stands but the boats which served them have gone to the waterways museums. Now pleasure boats come this way exploring the Weaver valley after the Anderton Lift was reopened on Jubilee Day.

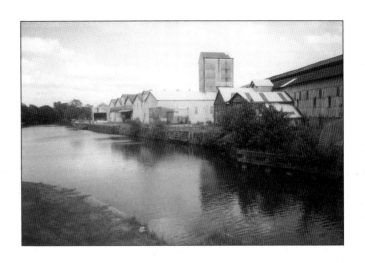

Across the river from Winnington stands Anderton Lift, built in the same year as the works. The canal had been taken so close to the river because James Brindley conceived a link with the Weaver there. The 'tips' on each side were where salt was dropped into waiting boats on the river from the canal, hence the nickname of the nearby pub 'The Tip'. In 2002, the lift was reopened and a union jack flies from the end to mark it. In the foreground is the special vessel purchased to take visitors on a trip through the lift, named *Edwin Clarke* in honour of the designer of the lift. The lift went into full use on Jubilee Day, 6 June 2002.

Barnton was one of the first places locally where workers were given mortgages to buy their own homes. Less fortunate people said they were so much in debt they could afford nothing but 'jam butties' to eat and people still say they are 'goin' up th'ill ter Jam Town'. Seen from the river, Barnton crowns the hill by the Weaver Navigation with an air of Victorian confidence. The hill has hardly changed, although more trees line the canal. The view is from outside the abandoned chemical works on Wallerscote Island.

To get the canal from Anderton to Runcorn – where the Duke of Bridgewater could charge to use the link on his canal to the Mersey – it was necessary to construct tunnels at Barnton, Salterford and Preston Brook. This was not an easy option to a link at Anderton! The Duke ordered that the tunnels were built six inches narrower than the Weaver river boats so they could never use them! This evocative picture was taken during winter frosts when boats could not pass. The tunnels today give a canal trip an air of mystery, as at times you can't see light at the other end!

Roads improved after the creation of County Councils in the 1880s and helped fuel a craze for cycles. At first they were penny-farthings, where the pedal turned the big wheel. However, the invention of the chain drive allowed more modern-shaped bikes. Touring with a club was a fashion which lasted until after the Second World War, and these Barnton bikers are about to set off on a day's tour. The building was given by John Brunner to be used as a village hall to mark the Jubilee and was opened in 1898. For a time it was used as an extra school for the village but is now used as the village hall again.

Posted in 1905, this card shows a view of Marbury Hall looking over the Mere. It was a grand house with a long tradition of hunting and of being a great social centre for the local 'upper class' people. There are many romantic stories about the place, including the Marbury lady and the Marbury Dunn – the first an illicit lover and the second a horse – both of which are said to haunt it. Today, sailing boats glide over the Mere on a sunny day and children come to try and spot the lady or the horse. The house is no more.

Marbury was rebuilt in the mid Victorian period as a French château in the style of Fontainebleu Palace. The setting of a huge park on the edge of the Salt Country and the famous collection of ancient marble statues collected in the eighteenth century ensured it was one of the most stately of local stately homes, employing a whole squadron of servants to ensure it ran smoothly. It was used for a variety of military purposes during the Second World War, and the barracks were used to house Polish refugees until they could be more properly housed. Today, the County Council maintain the grounds as a public country park.

Back to Winnington Hill. Only the offices on the right of this picture survive, and even they have lost the gas light and the grim spiked fence which was put there to prevent loitering in the shelter of the projecting corner. Many older buildings have corners cut away to improve the view of oncoming traffic. On the left, the old Town Bridge can be seen. All the buildings on the corner have been demolished and the council has purchased the piece of land next to the bridge intending to develop a green space to provide a clear view of traffic for drivers.

The old Town Bridge caused delays on the river as 'flatt' boats had to take down their masts to pass under it. This was inconvenient in an age when the Weaver Trustees were in fierce competition for trade with the railway lines. It was removed and the two long riveted metal sides were moved on barges to a new home, and now form the Victoria Bridge over the Dane (seen in the modern picture). The creation of the new crossings allowed traffic to use an alternative if the Town Bridge should break down at any time.

The new swing bridge, opened in 1899, allowed barges in full sail to pass through it in just two minutes. It is a remarkable structure which is cantilevered from the side with many iron weights underneath as a counter balance. To resist the subsidence effects, it rests on a floating pontoon so that the entire weight is supported by air floating in water. It is very rare for it to be opened today, but it still can be. The tow path, where elegant ladies once walked in long skirts, is now developed as a cycle track and walkway to link Winsford and Runcorn waterside.

The arches which support the bridge are higher on the Winnington side of the river to put more weight on the shorter side of the main support. Winnington Hill, with its white cottage, can be seen over the bridge, while the black and white Sportsman's Hotel is on the left, behind the gates which prevented accidents when the bridge was open. Today, there is almost non-stop traffic over the bridge but the black and white buildings add to the picturesque aspect.

To ensure that traffic would always be able to cross the river, a second bridge was built named after the France Hayhurst family of Bostock. If one bridge jammed, the other could be used to cross the river. Above it is Highfield House, built for Leader Williams, Surveyor to the Weaver Navigation and later the engineer who constructed the Manchester Ship Canal. Castle Church, near the site of the fort, was built for the use of men on the river boats.

Northwich brine baths were built in Verdin Park, with the Victoria Infirmary next to it, in the former house of Robert Verdin. They were all given to the town in 1887 when he was the Conservative MP. He died the following year. The inscription reads 'Cleanliness is next to Godliness' to emphasise they were for medical as well as pleasurable use. The gun came from the Crimean War. Although the statue still stands, the baths were destroyed by subsidence and the gun went for 'munitions' in the Second World War.

The Albert Infirmary was given to Northwich at the same time as the park with the aim of prevention as well as cure. Patients would benefit from the fresh air and from exercise in the park and baths, while the healthy could be encouraged to stay that way by using the facilities in the park. Verdin purchased a stone-clad house of Georgian character for the infirmary, and while it is not used for patients any more, it is a handsome administrative building where patients can sit in the gardens on a summer day.

Cameras turned out in droves when Castle Chambers collapsed in 1891. In fact, in this photograph the camera has recorded another photographer at work. On the right you can see the heavy canvas cover which allowed him to focus through the lens before putting in the glass plate to take the picture. Notice how the women maintain a polite distance behind him. Today the site is unrecognisable as a new development opened in 2002 replaced a garage which long occupied the site. The buildings are, of course, strongly reinforced – just in case!

Advertising was almost a Victorian invention and they revelled in it, as can be seen on this wall. Although the postcard view was taken to show the state of the road, between the houses can be seen the backyards and a privy, a reminder that this was once a warren of houses for workers in the salt works or on the river. Although this photograph is captioned Castle Street, it does not seem to match maps of the period. Perhaps the photographer mixed it with Chesterway? The modern photograph shows the side of Castle Street cleared for redevelopment.

Castle Church was built for the Weaver boatmen and sits on a cliff overlooking the town. It is well worth climbing the track up Highfield Hill for a fine view of Northwich and the Cheshire Peak District. Our cyclist would only have the view on Sunday as the smoke filled the valley for the rest of the week. Much early nineteenth-century housing was built over the Roman fort on Castle to be away from the smoke, and from the 1960s development has replaced the housing while archaeologists have rescued information about the fort.

49

PARRS-BANK-NOV 25 1891-N 86

In 1891 barges could, and did float under the Dane Bridge in London Road. Boating was a late Victorian and Edwardian passion and people were able to hire one on the river to spend a leisurely afternoon. The black and white building housed Parr's Bank. The Warrington bankers opened their Northwich branch after financing the foundation of Winnington Works. You would have to lie flat on a raft to pass under the Dane Bridge today as subsidence has lowered all that area of town. The buildings close to it are all provided with stepped entrances to keep the floors above the level of flooding. The floating hotel on the right avoids such problems!

In 1897 London Road was decked with flags and an arch at the entrance to the Brockhurst estate of the Verdin family to welcome the Duke of Westminster – Britain's richest man – to open the new Technical Schools. Model ideal housing for the estate can be seen through the arch which was much larger and more pleasant than any worker's housing in town. The estate housing still exists, although Brockurst Park was developed for housing over the years. Where the arch stood are traffic lights and a new road takes heavy traffic away from the residential area of Leftwich.

The great and important of Mid Cheshire were assembled outside the Verdin Technical Schools on 14 July 1897 to see the Duke and Duchess of Westminster open the Verdin Technical Schools with a golden key. A huge procession of them had paraded from Brockhurst through Northwich and back beforehand. The building is still used today by the Mid Cheshire College for some of its art classes, but most further education takes place in a large purpose-built college at Hartford. Access to this end of The Crescent was closed when the new road system was created.

ervants outside the Brockhurst. Their dress tells us who they were, in aprons and a hat are the maids, an apron but no hat denotes the housekeeper, while a hat and no apron is the lady's maid. A woman without an apron but wearing a feathered hat is the governess. The men are grooms, except the butler standing with a top hat by an informally dressed member of the family. There were no servants on hand when the modern photograph was taken, but the exterior of the building is largely unchanged. Inside, it is converted into luxury flats and the mosaic floor, presented by Edward VII when he visited, still survives.

Close to the Technical schools, the Weaver was lined with boat yards which made river vessels, even small sea-going ships, and repaired vessels when necessary. This array of river craft were most probably in for repairs or tied up for Sunday when there was no trade on the river so that the men could go to church. Northwich was known as an inland port then. There are still boat yards on the Weaver and this dramatic view of a flying barge (actually being lifted on a crane) was taken from the river.

Double locks allowed for the passage of small boats and barges while larger ships could use a bigger lock and were created in response to competition from the railways in the 1870s. Behind the large 'flatt boat' is a small cock boat which was pulled behind for use as a lifeboat in the tricky crossing of the Mersey. The modern view from a barge in the lock was taken after the Anderton Lift reopened giving access to the river again.

Lock and Viaduct. Northwich.

A view of the Northwich viaduct from the edge of the town. This is known as the Old River, a meander cut off when the Weaver was improved. The two iron sections were ordered by the Navigation trustees when the railway was extended to Chester. They could be removed to allow very tall vessels to pass and are like earlier ones over the Weaver at Frodsham. Today, swans swim and rushes grow in what is now Marshall's Arm Nature Reserve.

London Road runs parallel to the Weaver through Leftwich. There is no busy traffic on the road, but pedestrians and even a small flock of sheep can be seen by a gas street lamp. Today, the impression is very different. The houses are the same but each garden has been replaced by a parking bay. Even though most of the busy traffic into and out of Northwich has been diverted through the Kingsmeed Estate since the 1990s, London Road is still too busy for on street parking.

LEFTWICH GREEN

Davenham, Northwich.

We pause at Davenham – 'proud, poor but pretty', so the local saying goes – to see the church spire in the distance. It vies with the old tree at Bostock for the distinction of being the centre of Cheshire. By 1897, despite the motto, it was becoming a prosperous suburb of Northwich and now that the traffic has been diverted it is returning to this idyll. After almost a century of heavy traffic passing through the heart of the village, a second bypass was opened recently to link the pre-war bypass to Winsford around the village, but roadside parking continues in Church Street.

Bostock Hall was enlarged and decorated in Victorian and Edwardian times so as to be one of the grandest houses in the area. The money came from the family's interests in the trade on the Weaver. At this time it employed over 100 servants, many of whom lived in the house or on the model estate village which was rebuilt to improve the environment, besides providing homes for staff. In order to keep it standing, the interior of the hall was developed as luxury apartments while the splendid painted canvas ceilings were taken into the care of the Manchester Art Gallery.

The Bull Ring in Middlewich even included the Town Hall meeting room in Victorian times. The narrow streets surrounding the Church date back to the days of the Civil War when soldiers fought there. A gas lamp stands in front of one of a number of butcher's shops which in the past centred around the Bull Ring for obvious reasons. Today they have all gone, although a shop front with a bull's head has been retained. The site was developed as a setting for the town war memorial, although it caused controversy when created and was said to resemble a small zoo!

A horse-drawn showman's caravan from the fair, not a Gypsy, was passing down Hightown when this photograph was taken. On the left is the Town Hall, this stands on the site of its medieval predecessor which consisted of a council chamber reached by a ladder above an open sided butter market. In ancient times this was known as King's 'Mexom' or rubbish dump! Today, the area is used as a convenient parking space for people using the shops and supermarkets there as through traffic uses new wider roads on the other side of the church.

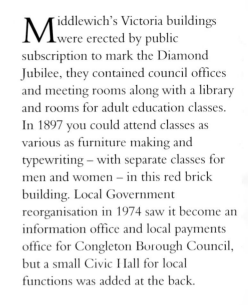

Middlewich's Victoria buildings were erected by public subscription to mark the Diamond Jubilee, they contained council offices and meeting rooms along with a library and rooms for adult education classes. In 1897 you could attend classes as various as furniture making and typewriting – with separate classes for men and women – in this red brick building. Local Government reorganisation in 1974 saw it become an information office and local payments office for Congleton Borough Council, but a small Civic Hall for local functions was added at the back.

A feature of canal-side Middlewich used to be pubs with upstairs and downstairs bars. Those entered from the front door were of a better class than those entered from the canal side, which offered boatees more basic facilities. The Navigation stood at the corner of Mill Lane by the Town Bridge, which can be seen beyond the policeman. A formidable woman is in the downstairs entrance; she looks like a landlady who will not accept bad behaviour. All the old houses and shops in this part of town were demolished over the years to

provide a clear way through for traffic. As a result, Middlewich is more often driven through than visited.

Fred H. Crosley lamented the changes taking place in Middlewich fifty years ago, claiming that it was fast becoming an ordinary industrial town to be avoided. Here is the old town that he remembered, seen from the Holmes Chapel Road. It was a picturesque jumble of old buildings with smoking chimneys and interesting alleyways, dominated by the old church. Now, road widening allows the M6 traffic to pass through Middlewich quickly and trees line the road. It is best to match the photographs by looking at the church tower and decide which, if any, you prefer.

It is almost impossible to say exactly where most pictures of salt making were taken. This one has been included because, unusually, it has a caption that says exactly where it was taken. Men are working half naked by the steaming pans finishing the lump salt. Murgatroyd's closed their salt works and concentrated on chemical manufacture nearer to Sandbach. The modern picture was taken inside British Salt's factory, where one man pushing a button can do the work of a whole factory full of his Victorian counterparts.

ISHING LUMP SALT.
RGATROYD'S SALT WORKS, MIDDLEWICH.

Seddon's salt works by the canal at Middlewich prospered as an independent company when most other salt works were joined to form the Salt Union which eventually closed down all the small works that joined it. This works was considered unimportant and unprofitable until the discovery of fresh supplies of brine made it a serious competitor. A fine model of the works was made before it was demolished and is now in the Salt Museum at Northwich. The area has been developed for canal-side housing with moorings for visitors to the town.

The Big Lock, by the Roman fort in Middlewich, is a reminder that the original plan was to join the Trent and Mersey to the Weaver at Northwich or Winsford so that sailing barges could reach Middlewich's salt works. It is the only lock on the canal big enough to take a sailing barge. At the turn of the century there was a canal-side bar and a small shop for the boat people. The downstairs part of the pub was a little taproom for people on the canal to use during the day while the upstairs became a more comfortable lounge bar for locals in the evening until the 1980s. Today, the entire building, including the former stables, caters for the boat trade during the summer.

On the outskirts of Winsford, Sir William Henry Verdin gave his home at Highfield House to become the Albert Infirmary as a belated Jubilee gift in 1899. Long-skirted and aproned nurses, serving maids and doctors posed for this opening photograph. It was placed to serve both Winsford and Middlewich. The old infirmary was demolished when Leighton Hospital was opened and later replaced by a modern purpose built home for the elderly where nurses in trousers and residents were photographed taking the sun.

From Winsford station to Salterswall was more or less just one long street with a few short streets to the side. The Wharton side of the river was developed for workers housing during the nineteenth century. A woman and child are at the centre of this picture by the old Primitive Methodist Chapel in Station Road which was taken in 1892 to record future damage which might be caused by subsidence. Close comparison of the two photos shows the rebuilding that has taken place but how much was due to salt subsidence and how much to 'home improvements' is difficult to say.

Like all the salt towns, Winsford had its share of street corner pubs, often no more than a cottage with room to serve beer (but not spirits) as allowed by The Beerhouses Act.

This was Wharton's Blue Bell, (not to be confused with the pub by Over Church). Next to it is a tiny shop, no more than a converted front room with a shop window providing daily essentials to local customers. The whole area has been cleared today and shoppers go to supermarkets rather than little shops and to big lounge bars, not corner beer houses.

A row of terraced cottages with Flemish brick fronts in Crook Lane, so called because it has a bend – not because of illegal habits! Much of the housing in Winsford was of a reasonable standard for the time with large gardens for growing vegetables, but with the Depression years of the twentieth century it became overcrowded and neglected. The modern photograph shows how, since the Second World War, the older property of Winsford has been altered to present a modern aspect and a continental look which obscures all traces of the original appearance.

The Verdin Brine Baths were built on the side of Winsford Flashes to provide indoor swimming with salty water. It was not just for exercise, the brine baths of Mid Cheshire had the reputation of a spa and, besides fit people coming to exercise, invalids would bathe in brine to relieve various ailments. Fire destroyed the baths and the area of the old dockyard has been developed into a pretty marina with facilities for children to paddle canoes and feed the swans. A modern swimming pool serves the town near the shopping centre.

On the other side of the road, the Ark was just one of over half a dozen hotels and beerhouses in the market place area of Winsford which served both the salt workers, who would call in after work or would have beer taken to the workplace, and also men from the boats. Today the area near the bridge is still the town's night spot with music and dancing until the early hours. The Ark remains a fine example of local building techniques with half timbered construction outside and plank lined walls to resist subsidence inside, it is probably the only building in Winsford to retain these original details.

The Town Hall and Market Hall were operated by the same company. Winsford was one of the earlier generation of town halls which were assembly rooms where social events and meetings were held, not council offices. A salt barge is anchored by the town bridge, while the structure on the left is the hoist from which goods were taken from boats into the Co-op. Today, all of this has vanished to be replaced by a pleasant wooded area which separates the two parts of the town. It was felt better to replace the old town centre which was endangered by subsidence and flooding with a new safer one up the hill.

As late as the 1960s a large part of what was purchased in Winsford came from the Co-op shops. This group occupied the 'bottom of Winsford', so called because every way to it came down a hill. The shops have sunk below the road level, which has been raised to keep it level after subsidence. They were all replaced over the next couple of decades by buildings which lasted until the town development of the late 1960s when they were all closed and replaced by a department store on the shopping centre. That did not last long and the Co-op presence in Winsford all but disappeared during the '70s.

The bottom of Winsford might well have been an apt name, for few places were more dismal 100 years ago when Fletcher Moss passed through what he termed 'the vilest hole'. The air was thick with smoke from chimneys mixed with the steam from over 1,000 pans of boiling brine. This was compounded by the odour of rotting meat from the bone and fertiliser works where animals unfit for consumption were processed. It has seen many changes in the twentieth century and now the only building left is the old post office building, now a chip shop.

You could not go down the road which now takes lorries to the Salt Mine, called New Road, as it was only built after the Salt Mine reopened in 1928. To get to Northwich and beyond people took a train along the Cheshire Lines railway or would beg a lift on one of the boats. Hardly anything grows on the site today as it was long used to store vast piles of crushed rock. From close to this spot the old railway has been converted to a country walkway and the area is being planted as woodland.

It was said the further up the High Street you lived, the better off you were. Mary Stoneley – presumably that is her in the doorway – kept the Fox and Hounds Inn near the bottom of the hill. Note the shuttered windows for safety! The sign is of interest as the emblem in the arch is a diagram of a section through a salt mine, the logo of Sandiford's Brewery in Northwich. Now the old road is a cul-de-sac only used occasionally by drivers to park overnight. Trees replace the pubs and shops of old and through traffic is diverted onto a new dual carriageway.

A prosperous new civic centre was planned in the late Victorian period, halfway up the hill in Over Lane, intended to be away from the smoke and the risk of floods and fires. It was an area where the Victorians could build substantial red brick buildings like other towns. The Guildhall was promised to the town to mark the Diamond Jubilee in 1897 but not completed until 1899 when the area became known as Guild Hall Square. Today, the red brick buildings survive and are used for similar purposes to the original donors' instructions.

The Verdins planned to open the Technical Schools in Northwich as a Diamond Jubilee gift, but built smaller ones in Winsford to act as a trial run so that any mistakes could be rectified in the final gift. If the Queen lived until 1897 it was to be a Diamond Jubilee gift, but if not could still mark her Golden Jubilee. It opened in 1894. Today the handsome terracotta structure is the town's adult education centre and is best known to many as the place where the buses stop for the shopping centre.

After women were forbidden to work by the salt pans in 1870, fustian cutting became an important job. The fustian was a sort of velvet woven in Manchester and was sent to parts of Cheshire for finishing. Women in Manchester had other choices of work but locally they were content to walk back and forth, cutting rows of loops with a sharp pointed knife. The factory was long used as a depot by Cheshire Fire Brigade which now has a main base in Winsford. The old mill in John Street was destroyed by fire and replaced by modern housing, but the date plaque of the building was retained and set into the wall.

In 1897 the chimney of the first Winsford Cotton Mill was still standing as a landmark despite most of the mill having been burnt to the ground in 1874. A crowd of children gathered on the ruins when it was demolished in 1904. In the background can be seen the John Street Mills where the fustian cutters were photographed. Today, an old people's home stands on the site but the modern picture shows what happened to the bricks – they were used to build the 'chimney houses' in Upper Haigh Street.

A jovial scene at Over Square or Four Lane Ends. Over had its own silver band, as did many of the local towns and organizations like the Salvation Army. In an age before recorded music, radio and television, the playing of instruments was an important part of working and middle class life. Men would join a military-style band, while girls learned to play the piano from an early age. The Old White Bear pub and the Over Brewery behind it have closed down and the pub is now a home. Traffic is so heavy in this part of Winsford that Over Square roundabout was built to ease problems. The joke is, of course, to point out that it is neither round nor square.

Looking back for a moment we see the entrance into Swanlow Lane. Even in Victorian times, a Dr Okel had a surgery there, in his house behind the wall on the left. The last one was practising until the 1960s. The impressive Congregational Chapel and tiny cottage then stood in fields while the large house beyond was the Manse. The old thatched cottage, like many others in the area went as 'slum clearance' in the 1960s, and the old road is now used just for access to the chapel. Some of the old trees from the doctor's garden, including rhododendrons, still grow around the roundabout.

This must have been a fairly large timber-framed thatched farmhouse in the seventeenth century. One hundred years ago it was split into two parts, one a shop and the other the home of Mr A. Massey who ran the shop. It also served as a smallholding, with a shippon for five cattle, a dairy, piggery, hen pen and stabling for three horses, plus 'a good garden and orchard'. The house was replaced by three small shops in 1973 when old timber was used in converting Knights Grange into pub. The tree has grown since then!

As the road passes out of Salterswall and under the old railway line to the salt works, an arch beyond 'the wishing seat' (actually the remains of a thirteenth-century cross) leads to Marton Hall Farm. On the right is the moat of Marton Grange, where the half-timbered Tudor hall stood until 1848. The island in the moat still remains, but is hidden by the trees which surround the water, apart from a bit used for ducks in the farm yard. The moat can best be seen from the Whitegate Way following the old railway line.

L ord Delamere retained much of the half-timbered architecture on his estate, but hired the brilliant local architect John Douglas to modernise it for him. The old thatched cottage by Whitegate village green is a good example of a building where old timber was retained where possible. A new front wall was provided and tall chimneys, on Jacobean lines, were added. This house had an even stranger history in the twentieth century when it was separated into two tiny dwellings. Each was sold and developed separately so that today two modern homes are joined by a seventeenth-century cottage.

Lord Delamere spent much of the late Victorian and Edwardian periods developing white settlements in Kenya. His ancestral home at Vale Royal was let to tenants, including the American millionaire Mr Dempster, who financed excavations of the abbey church there. The Cheshire Hunt are assembling outside in the old photograph, while the modern picture shows the house restored as the club house at the centre of a modern golf course and an historic apartment block.

The Round Tower at Sandiway was part of a romantic entrance to the Vale Royal estates. From there, the carriage road crossed the park to pass the Monkey Lodge and make for the house over what is now golf courses. The tower was a decorative lodge for the gatekeeper, which can clearly be seen in the old photograph, while to the left a steam lorry chugs up the hill. Today, people travelling along the Manchester to Chester road are often puzzled by what on earth it could be, as it was retained in 1938 as a feature when the dual carriageway was created and as Sandiway's mark of the Millennium and Jubilee it was restored in 2002.

It is uncertain who these men dressed up in their Sunday best outside the Blue Cap at Sandiway are, yet Victorian class distinction is quite clear in that most who wear a hat, wear a flat cap. Only one is wearing a bowler hat and is presumably the leader of the group; to the left a man in a trilby does not look as if he is in the party. Perhaps they have stopped on an outing? While it attracted walkers and cyclists a century ago, the Blue Cap has evolved into a large hotel complex with restaurants and accommodation on the busy main road. A life-sized model of the hound, Blue Cap, (which won 500 guineas in a race) stands on a sign outside.

Hefferston Grange, seen on the way into Weaverham, stood in park land. Before the start of the First World War, the daughter of the house, Robina Heath, eloped on her bike to Gretna Green to marry the garden boy she had been forbidden to see. Rather than let her inherit, her father sold the house and lands to Warrington Corporation to establish a tuberculosis sanatorium there. The house and grounds have been redeveloped in recent years and a modern fence prevents an exactly duplicate photo being taken. The development, unfortunately, destroyed a splendid eighteenth-century plaster ceiling depicting Roman emperors.

Hefferstone Grange, Weaverham

The road through Weaverham shows a four-wheeled farm wagon and children standing outside one of the village's half-timbered cottages in the middle of the road. At the turn of the century it was a little self-contained village and amongst the local craftsmen was the undertaker, wheelwright and joiner whose home at Poplar Cottage juts into the road in the distance. Although the buildings are still the same today, the Wheatsheaf pub has been painted white and it is hardly safe to stand in the road where a zebra crossing and double yellow lines prevent parking – even to take a photograph!

Like most parish churches, Weaverham church had a pub at the gates. In Victorian times, the Ring o'Bells gained a certain notoriety when the Virgin's Club, a group of women who marched to the church of The Virgin Mary, immaterial of marital status, would leave their service and go and drink too much at this pub. The event was stopped, however. The pub's licence was moved to a new building at the other end of the village to serve the new housing development at Owley Wood and the site then provided a car park for the church in 1924.

The tower of Hartford church was added in 1889. Victorian attention to comfort is seen in the vestry with a chimney away from the main road, indicating that a boiler house is underground for the heating system. Hartford became a popular place for tradesmen and for managers from the Winnington works to move to, away from Northwich. The handsome church building was constructed by John Douglas to serve the prosperous village of Hartford and it is, for the most part, unchanged outside. Of the interior the architect Pevsner wrote 'almost everything is of interest'. However, changes in worship have seen much of what impressed him totally removed.

An old story goes that when Hartford church was opened in 1875, an old woman complained about being 'forced to sit between a salt boiler and a soap maker'. On investigation it turned out that they were none other than Sir Joseph Verdin and Sir Joseph Crosfield. She came from a 'county' family and their money came from trade – hence the social division! Today the church has a thriving congregation who have built the extension to the tower and opened a second place of worship in the old Greenbank station. The extension makes no pretensions to being original work.

On the river bank, fashionable ladies walk along the towpath on a sunny afternoon by the old single-arched stone bridge at Hartford. It is difficult to believe that this scene was in the heart of the Salt Country. It must have been on a Sunday when traffic on the river was forbidden, as there are no boats visible and ladies would certainly not have walked there when rough boatmen were passing. In the summer of 2002, this length of the river was reopened to allow holiday boats to pass up to Winsford again. The 'new' bridge of 1938 can be lifted a further ten feet to allow ships to pass, but the only ones to do so today are holiday barges.